Pebble® Plus

Investigate the Seasons

Let's Look at Winter

Revised Edition

Download the Capstone 4D app for additional content.

4D See page 2 for directions.

by Sarah L. Schuette

CAPSTONE PRESS
a capstone imprint

Download the Capstone 4D app!

- Ask an adult to search in the Apple App Store or Google Play for "Capstone 4D".
- Click Install (Android) or Get, then Install (Apple).
- Open the app.
- Scan any of the following spreads with this icon:

When you scan a spread, you'll find fun extra stuff to go with this book!
You can also find these things on the web at www.capstone4D.com
using the password: **winter.08451**

Pebble Plus is published by Capstone Press,
1710 Roe Crest Drive, North Mankato, Minnesota 56003
www.mycapstone.com

**Library of Congress Cataloging-in-Publication Data
is available on the Library of Congress website.**

ISBN 978-1-5435-0845-1 (library binding)
ISBN 978-1-5435-0873-4 (paperback)
ISBN 978-1-5435-0877-2 (ebook pdf)

Editorial Credits

Sarah Bennett, designer; Tracy Cummins, media researcher,
Laura Manthe, production specialist

Photo Credits

Shutterstock: Africa Studio, 5, Bakusova, 19, Dieter Hawlan,
1, FotoRequest, Cover, Jeff Thrower, 17, Jim Cumming, 13,
Khomulo Anna, 3, Liubou Yasiukovich, Cover Design Element,
Marina Zezelina, 9, Ondrej Prosicky, 15, Peter Wey, 21,
SnvvSnvvSnvv, 7, tim elliott, 11

Note to Parents and Teachers

The Investigate the Seasons set supports national science
standards related to weather and life science. This book
describes and illustrates the season of winter. The images
support early readers in understanding the text. The repetition
of words and phrases helps early readers learn new words. This
book also introduces early readers to subject-specific vocabulary
words, which are defined in the Glossary section. Early readers
may need assistance to read some words and to use the Table of
Contents, Glossary, Read More, Internet Sites, Critical Thinking
Questions, and Index sections of the book.

Printed in the United States of America.
010773S18

Table of Contents

It's Winter!

How do you know it's winter?

The temperature is cold.

The ground hardens.

Water freezes.

When snow falls,

it covers everything.

The sun rises later
in the morning.
Winter days are
the shortest of the year.

Animals in Winter

What do animals do
in winter?
Deer search for food
under the snow.

Some brown rabbits turn white.

Now their fur blends in

with the snow.

Owls sit in snowy trees.

They stay

for the whole winter.

Some birds migrate.

Plants in Winter

What happens

to plants in winter?

They do not grow.

Many plants look bare

and brown.

Evergreen trees stay green.

They keep their needles

all year round.

What's Next?

The temperature gets warmer.

Winter is over.

What season is next?

Glossary

bare—not covered

evergreen—a tree or bush that has green needles all year long

freeze—to become solid or icy at a very low temperature

migrate—to move from one place to another when seasons change

needle—a sharp, green leaf on an evergreen tree

season—one of the four parts of the year; winter, spring, summer, and fall are seasons

temperature—the measure of how hot or cold something is

Read More

Phillips, Dee. *Snowshoe Hare.* Arctic Animals. New York: Bearport Publishing, 2015.

Rustad, Martha E. H. *All About Animals in Winter.* Celebrate Winter. North Mankato, Minn.: Capstone Press, 2016.

Ward, Jennifer. *What Will Grow?* New York: Bloomsbury, 2017.

Internet Sites

Use FactHound to find Internet sites related to this book.

Visit *www.facthound.com*

Just type **9781543508451** and go.

 Check out projects, games and lots more at
www.capstonekids.com

Critical Thinking Questions

1. How does white fur help some rabbits in winter?

2. What happens to the days in winter?

3. Describe what you like to do in winter.

Index